The Boy Who Would Be Sage

Poems on the Life of Ramana Maharshi

Ana Ram Callan

DEDICATION

For my cherished Ramana, whose love transcends all language

INTRODUCTION

I n July 2000, after a profound accident which involved a near death experience, I was given a gift of a session with a spiritual teacher, David Waldman. It turned out to be the gift of my life. I began attending meditation sessions and retreats with him, at first lying on the floor at his feet. "There is nothing you have to do," he said. And I knew I'd come to the right place for my battered body was incapable of doing anything.

At our first retreat in Mexico, I was intoxicated with the wild beauty of the place - vibrant flowers, soft ocean, wide open sky delighted me after such a dark time. A man spoke during the Question and Answer period. In my haze, all I heard was, "Praise God." Something erupted inside, an explosion in the chest. For the first time, the truth of that simple statement was patently clear. It seemed there was nothing else to do but sing hymns of praise to every aspect of God's creation. I stumbled through the desert, sometimes on my hands and knees, intoxicated by the cactus, the jeweled sand, the braying donkey. Smitten with the dream world, I cried for hours, tears of gratitude for this miracle of life. Even the pain in my broken body felt beautiful. I was In Love for the first time, and it felt natural as air.

One evening soon after, I was looking at a photograph of Ramana Maharshi on the altar - of whom I knew little - when all of a sudden, He airlifted into my heart. Literally.

It was as if the shattering of the world as I had known it had freed up space for Him, for True Love. I had never imagined such bounty. Every breath, every second, every sound seemed sacred, my entire being imbibing of His feast.

For ten years, I left the world while Ramana - and David - carried me through a dark night of the soul, freeing all the old baggage that I had lumbered around with for lifetimes. It was a supremely exquisite and torturous time. Never did I doubt that the wisdom and compassion of the Sage would hold me.

I began to read stories of Ramana's life: his birth in Tirichuzi, India, in 1879; his awakening as a teenager; his pilgrimage to his guru, Holy Mountain Arunachula; his many years of silence and meditation; the ashram that formed around Him. I was enamored of and awed by His profound love and respect for every creature, flower, tree.

Each story I read seemed to leap off the page; it was as if Ramana took me into the most intimate reaches of His dream being. I felt as if I were actually there, witness to these amazing tales. And pen would float to paper soon afterwards to record it. The result is this book you now hold in your hand.

Ramana died in 1950, at the age of 70, His left arm riddled with sarcoma. He refused all medication, bearing the wounds of the world in His lustrous form. His entire life devoted to the well being of all. I read once that God gathered the dust from the feet of His devotees and made a shrine of it, doing *puja* or worship to it. God - the most humble of all - embodied in Ramana's selfless life. May His limitless love whisper to you too.

Poem
One

❧ One ❧

When His love flowers through,
I am hopeless but to be His lover,
arms fondling every tress
of his creation – the lid
of garbage cans is Him,
plastic flowers I have to kiss,
helpless to resist His
Heaven-scented beauty,
tongue, heart, lips
licking tendril clouds,
used-up leaves, mislaid
rings for keys, all of it
is He, He whispers
through the reeds,
In every single thing,
find me. And I do,
stroking, rocking,
holding lost parts
of his body, fear
and loss and greed,
bullets, blame,
disease, all of it
His holy kingdom,
of which I am a vassal
and a fool, stupid
with love for Him,
beguiled, besotted,
smitten with the dream
of His entire Being.

CONTENTS

I

VENKATARAMAN

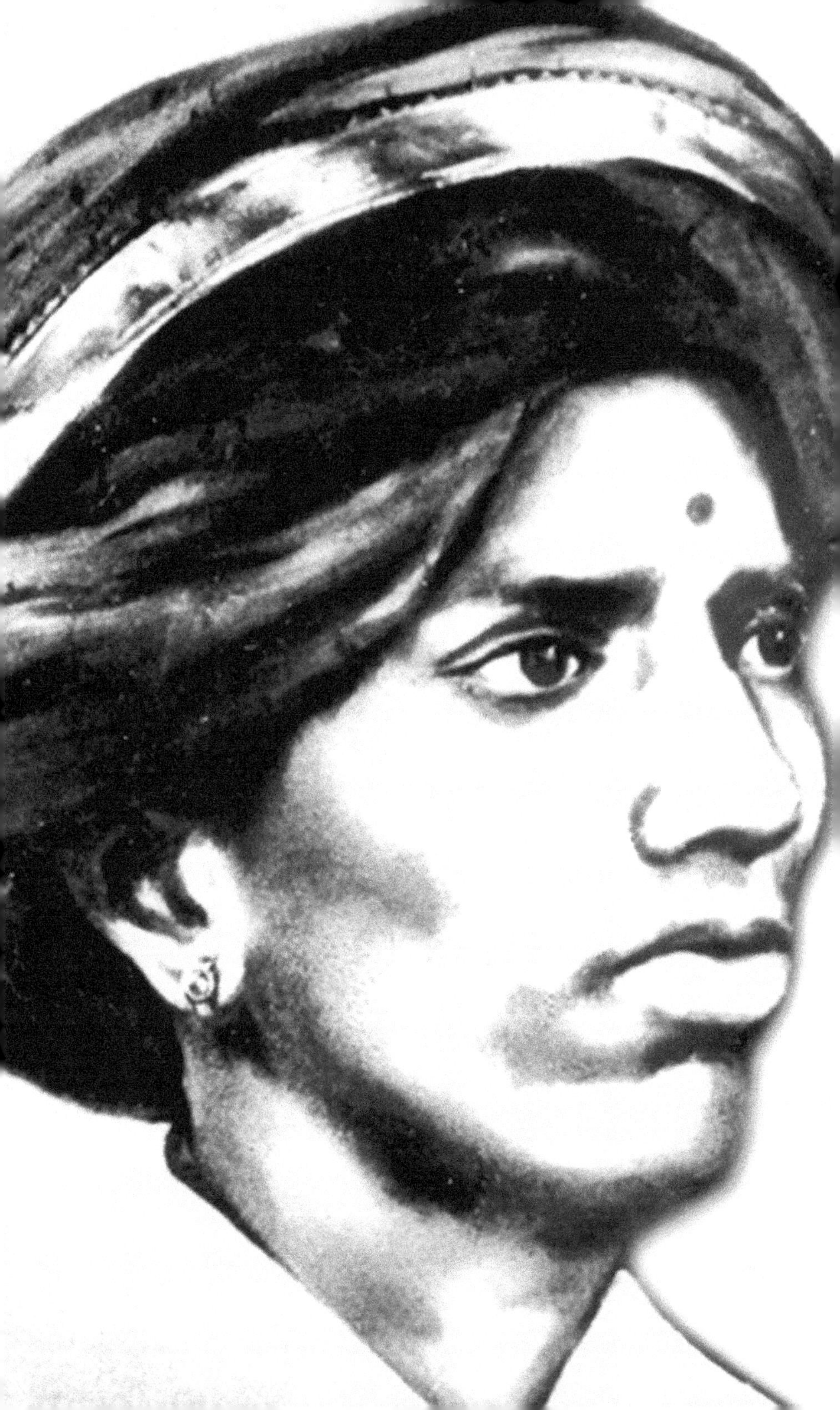

Father of
The Village

Even the thieves laid down
their wares when he appeared,
humbled into submission
by the heft of his kindness.
He who heard the wounds
of his tribe and held them
who made peace from others'
differences, whose door
was always open, bed always
offered, who took the hungry
and the lost and fed them
love, a feast they could suckle
on and remember kindness,
justice, warmth. The man
who could heal loneliness
with his steady calm, whom
rajas and magistrates would
bow to, whose wife was priceless
pearl, whose son, fashioned
by the gods, flowed through
them, to become the One
Father Of the World.

Alagammal

Pearl Beyond Price
Jewel Beyond Rubies
Mother of the Mystic
whose human beliefs
and needs would melt
with every meal she cooked,
every chant she sung,
every way she bowed
to the Master, her
second son, who
named her Beautiful,
and gave his lap to her
so she could blossom
out of her body,
scattering petals
of devotion and *pappadum*
into
The One Pure Heart
Of Love.

The Advent Of
❧ Venkataraman ☙

Exploding out of the center of the center
of the kernel of the sun, He took on form
for everyone. A rainbow merging light
and dark, He flew into our universe
to remind us of The One, the Only
Light of our True Being, the chance
to forever free the chains of needing,
He was born to bear the love
we were born out of and still long
for, a shimmering shuddering
boy-sage in the making, in
the conveyance of His mother
for nine months until the moon
was in position and the stars
arrayed in shimmering bouquets,
and sun o sun o sun waiting
to embody He Who Is Most Bright
to shine His infinite rays on
every finite one.

Golden Hands

They called Him
for everything He touched
was flooded with the sun -
His grandmother's soup
by the grace of His hand
tasted of angels,
every game He played
He won, every race,
everywhere He swum,
He came in first, He
Who Is the Origin,
who needs to prove
nothing, He whose
long, slender fingers
glow with the Divine
and even now, they
burnish and shine
as I hold them
o my god I stroke them
in my own.

After the Wedding

His uncle Subbier chastised
the boy for who knows
so He took his heaving
heart to the temple
of Sahayambal, Goddess
wise, and poured
His sorrows out before
her in a waterfall
of words and tears
until He was emptied
and could lie down
on cool, smooth stones,
stroked and soothed
by the True Mother.

Mischief Days By
❧ The Koundinya ❧

Sneaking in with His pals
to a place where trespassing
was not allowed, scaling
the back wall and leaping
down.

Bathing in the river, pouring
water over the holy Linga,
making food offerings
to the gods and then
relishing eating them.

Posing for a photograph,
large book placed in
His arms so He would
appear studious, but

just as the shutter
was about to click,
Ven raised his arm
to flick off a fly.

How can humans
label or contain
an unpredictable
saint in the making?

Boyhood Antics

I.

Venkata wove slippers
of twisted vines
to save His sister's feet
when they walked
from village to village
so the stones and pebbles
and stray twigs
would leave her
blisterless.

II.

Ven, a high caste Brahmin
chose Sab Jahan
to be His best friend
so Muslim and Hindu
could fuse
into a sacred whole,
a marriage in God
who knows
no differences.

III.

Ven sneaked up to the attic
and stole a sheaf
of His father's papers
then shared them
with His friends
who made boats of them
and sailed them on the river
but when His father found out,

he swore, "Strip my son
of his clothes and take him
from my house."
Ven left in haste
and could not be found
until dusk,
when it took a priest
lighting lamps
in the temple
to chance upon
a second statue,
still as stone,
hidden in a deep alcove,
who turned into
Venkataraman
and His father gleaned
hints of that boy's magic
and carried his son,
crowned victor,
on his heaving shoulders
home.

Deep Rest

Ven so deeply sleeping
even His family pounding
on the doors and windows
could not rouse Him
nor even the dozen boys
in Dindigal
pummeling His far-gone
flesh. Beaten blue and
red and black for hours,
He remained resting
where we all long
to go, in the painless
essence of His True Self.

❧ Who Is Nayana? ❧

After His father died,
Ven watched His mother
and brothers cry
and sat a long while
pondering the disguise
of death. Long hours,
He sat, examining
like a scientist
what this 'I" was.
It makes the body move,
He realized, noting
how His father's "I"
had left the flesh,
yet his Being
was not separate.
Baby steps in preparation
for His true enlightenment
four years on.

☙ Flawless ❧

The final vestiges of ego unthreading
themselves as He lay on His bed,
watching His flesh separate from
His breath, without flinching,
He let die what seemed dead,
and still, He watched, finding
Himself perfectly endless,
the little i having fled,
leaving only spaciousness,
silence swimming round
in His head, and the name
of His father graven into
His chest, as He rose,
sixteen years old, and mad
for His Master, the mountain,
He took off down the road,
barefoot, just a note to His
family amidst his schoolbooks,
foodless and famished for God,
whom He thought would leap
down from a tree and besiege
him, but it had already happened,
God himself implanted in each
cell of His being, no longer boy
but divinity supreme.

July 17, on the occasion of Venkataraman's awakening

II.

JOURNEY TO ARUNACHULA

ॐ August 29 ॐ

Time waits for no one but the saint
and so the train delayed until
Venkataraman came at midnight
to take His seat.
Leaving His home in Tirichuzi,
He traveled for three days
in the winnowing eaves of August.
A handful of rupees, heart full
of God, He followed the path
laid out for Him.
Lit from within, nothing
could stop Him, not hunger,
not fatigue, not fainting
on the ground, scattering
loose rice like wild seeds.
Not thirst, though no one
would offer Him water.
He was freeing the last
of his old life
- pears that could no longer feed,
two ruby earrings, every last
lock of His hair –
so He could arrive
empty.
Chilled to extremities,
He walked on, miles
piling up behind Him,
Arunachula now breathing
inside as He approached,
burning and hollowed.

The boy who would be sage
lay down before His father,
saying, "I have come,"
and the rains wept tears
of the gods for three days,
as they sang, "*Welcome,
My Own Son, Welcome.*"

Ghost

The boy leaping off a train,
racing through the streets,
His wind-whipped hair
a nest of coal and sapphire
is just an apparition;
the rice He almost starves for
and then spills, the teeming
rain, the thousand angels
singing are mere phantoms
conjured in our hearts
to know what's real:
the ruby earrings exchanged
for water, belongings tossed
aside are all illusion
guiding us as He was led
to the magnetic tide of love
swept towards itself –
boy to hill
sage to mountain
god to guru –
leaving us the one
uncompromising signature
of Truth.

✑ September 1 ✑

The packet of sweets,
the *dhoti*,
all attachments tossed
to the breeze
when He came
to the feet of his Father.
Bearing only the love
in His heart, limitless,
o so much larger
than anything
that can be owned.

❧ Magnet ❧

Cross-legged in a cave,
regardless of boys
stoning Him, oblivious
to the ants, vermin,
mosquitoes gnawing
His skin, blood,
pus, sweat dripping
out of Him
until two men came
and lifted His almost-
skeleton out
of the darkness
and still He remained
lost in God,
lost to the world,
a feather of flesh
and when they whispered
Gurumurtum,
He let
them raise and
carry Him to
the temple
where He would stare
inwards for years,
heedless
of time,
of garbled limbs,
serenaded by air
and seraphim
god-passion,
love-dust
shimmer-immer-immering.

Thank You Nayanar
and Tambiran

for tending our Holy Master,
seeing Him so emaciated, hollowed out,
bone thin, heart quakes and flails
and yet you held and looked after Him.
Thank you for taking care
of Our True One, Our Own, bless you,
holy men, for knowing the role that
would aid all creatures, human,
animal, divine. Thank you for your
lives and helping Him to go
where he had to.
Thank you, Temple Vehicles,
for sheltering His holy frame,
and ground for letting Him
move lizard-like, in a dream,
towards the bus that would
fit Him, He sitting under
its belly in the dark, the
quietest place He could find.
And thank you, Arali trees,
sweet scent of oleander
with your cut off branches
and leaves, for not scratching
Him as he crawled
in a trance through
your trimmed foliage.

We love you, ages on,
for your generous balm
offered to our King
of Kings, when
He seemed
to need it.

Days at
Gurumurtum

Palanaswami made a pillow
for his Master's flesh,
who reeled whenever He
tried to raise up on His haunches.
Hair clumped and wild,
hands useless but to reach for food,
He drank what was offered him
each night, a cup of mixed *prasad*,
caring nothing for the taste,
nails dangling off His jewel fingers,
It hurt, He said, to excrete,
but still He sat, heedless
to the world until they asked
where He came from,
for they saw His writing
on the wall, *Food is
the only service this body
requires*, they saw it written
in perfect Tamil and so
the questions grew
until Ven pointed
to a book on the ground
which held a story
based in His home town
and so they found
His family of origin.

Regardless, Ven stayed
in His cave, not uttering
a word, barely breathing,
never straying, looking
only inward
into the cave of His
perfect being.

❧ Baptism ❧

Ladies coming to wash Your hair
and bathe You, prepared with
nut soap and water, as You sat
immersed in frameless nectar
staring straight into forever
yet You let yourself be washed
and laughed years after at
the ladies' determination,
which You honored by offering
Your stainless body, always
entertaining others' needs
before Your own, perhaps
because You had none. Clean
or dun, matted or fresh-shaven,
You always have first claim
on Heaven's kingdom, on
whose fine hairs we hang
our hopes and offer slight
tokens of inexpressible
appreciation.

Mango Grove

Ramana sat perched like a bird,
at first, inside the tiny shed,
no room to even stretch His legs,
the roof a nest of twigs and leaves.
The farmer offered his mangoes
but Ramana refused,
waiting for the bats
to chew holes in them
and drop them on the roof,
('*Tut! Tut!*' was the noise
they made, He said)
which He would then
relish freely, receiving
true *prasad*
from the winged creatures
of the night,
whose droppings He lapped up
humbly, gleefully.

✿ Seed ❀

Ramana, on cold December nights,
His body caked in dirt,
would fold His legs up close
and tuck His head inside
His nest like a bird
and sink down slowly
into earth, and rest.
At dawn, His back emerged
in a shimmer of frost and dew,
mist pouring off His perfect skin,
a quilt of sunlight so pure,
surely flowers could grow out of Him.

Crownicure

Hair long and matted,
stones and twigs gathered there,
it hung heavy like a world of cares
and when someone
finally shaved Him,
his head felt so light,
He wondered if
it was still there
and kept shaking it
to make sure
it still existed,
so freed, He felt,
He said.

❧ Grace ❧

For years,
Ramana sat yielding
to the flow of God,
unyielding to the forces
of the world that come
and go
so when His family arrived
to take Him home,
He said,
I am already home
not in words or action
but by sitting like
His mountain Lord,
immovable and strong
until His family let go
of holding on
and they sat together
glorying in the forgotten
and true familiar face of God.

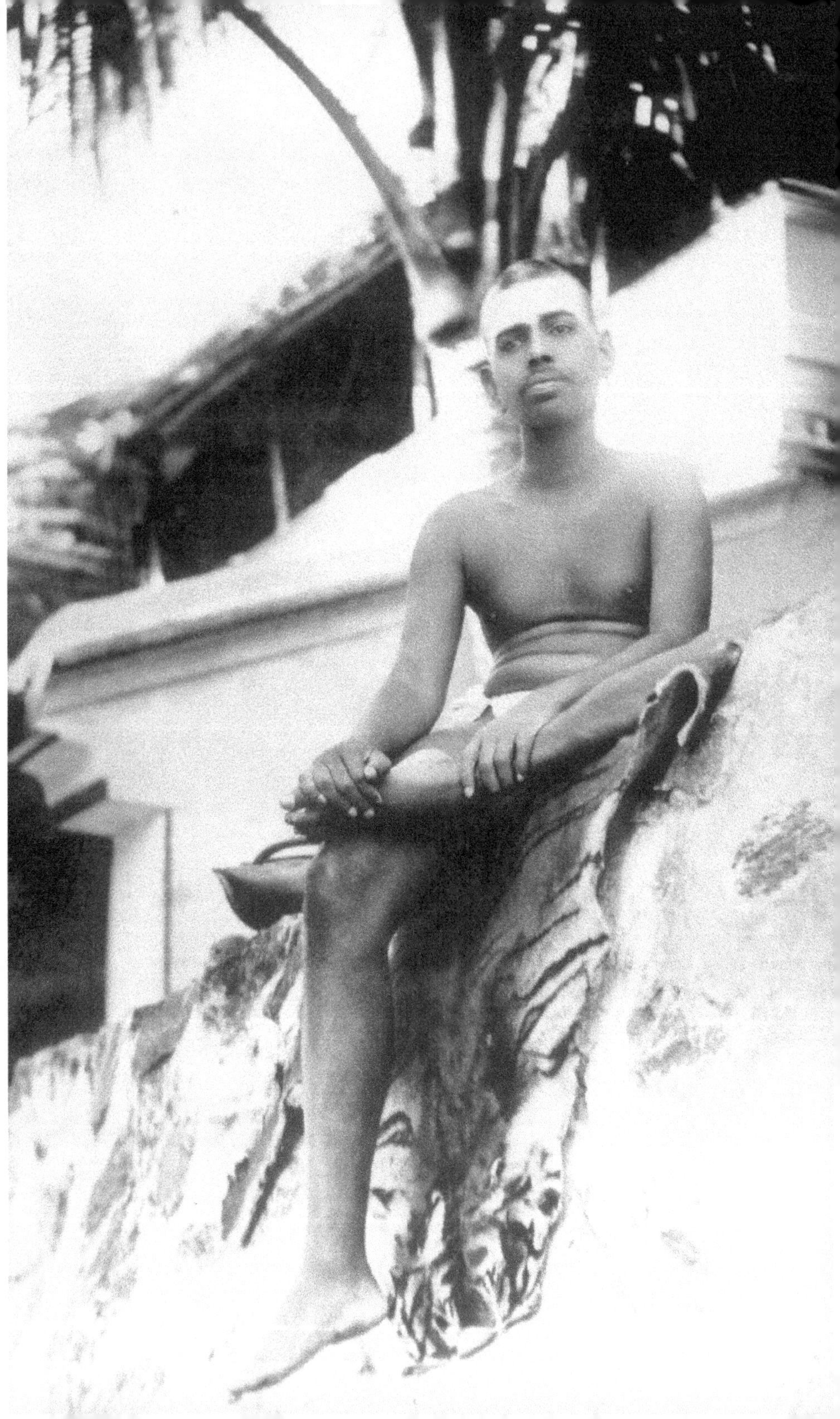

III.

SILENCE INTO WORDS

Brahmana Swami

The mouthless one.
He who lives above the clouds.
He through whose luminous eyes flow oceans.
Giver of illumination.
Singer of great silence.
Lover of divine in all humans.
Worshipped by dogs.
Adored by deer.
Widely licked by cows.
Animal god.
Master of birds.
King of all kings.
He without footprint.
Holiest of holies Brahman.

ᓓ Heart ᓓ

– In praise of Ganapati Muni

Out of the wordless space
He lured you.
His unspeakable devotion
earned the supreme reward:
grace of Your speech,
precise distillations
of the one true teaching.
The mouth of Heaven
opened when He spoke
offering the one word
Who? that would guide
each willing disciple
slowly, surely back
to the original fruit.

Asu Kavi

Ganapati Muni's gift

Shiva pours honey
in drops onto his tongue
and warm milk onto his quill
so every word that spills
out is liquid,
is cream dribbling
down the round peach
of his mouth, ripe
with truth, moist
with beauty,
filling the hearts
of his lovers
with pure food.

Nothing Is As It Appears

Before:
Through the valley of death,
the lone compass of I-I
guided Him through the mess
of what once was human,
laden with choice and
preferences.
After:
His palate yielded to this
food, or that, to love
or brutality, with indifference.
Before, His eyes were wide open
but what did He see?
During the end of the breath,
He pushed through the coldness,
the leaden flesh, to ask,
Who am I?
After, He sat for years,
eyes closed, absorbed
in The Answer.
When He opened them,
people reveled in His
changing form.

But He said, "you see
my body and think
I am that.
I tell you,
I am Brahman,
ever the same.
When I sat silent,
my lids were closed.
Now they are open.
That is the sole change."

❧ Love ❧

Finding Ramana on the hill
in rags, scrawny, foodless,
the boy's heart surged
with deep concern.
In loving earnest,
he leaned forwards,
whispering, *I have*
a good master. Let
me take you to him.
He'll feed you 3
pies a day, and if
you offer to help,
he might raise
it to six.
Ramana listened, heeding
such easy kindness
as the boy sat open-
palmed, head tilted
unknowingly towards
Brahman.

The Friend Of All

Wounded doves dropped out of the air
onto His feet.
Sparrows flew in to tell him of their quarrels.
Dogs paid no heed to their food
until He stopped to eat.
Such is the Majesty of One So Kind,
He Becomes All Creatures.
The deer received Him as their own.
Peacocks saw him and said, "Our kind."
Humans too could find
their perfect mirror
in His steady gaze,
His liquid eyes.
He loved them
without their even trying.
He honored, held and fed them all
until they felt complete:
the dog with ruptured insides,
the cow who bowed to Him,
pigs, squirrels, goats
all made a friend of Him.
He did not say, "I'm separate,"
so they didn't see it,
savoring instead the seamless love
that freed them,
every willing being invited
into God's own family.

✤ Ramana's Women ✤

The old lady slowly
lighting lamps in early evening,
her back curved like half a moon,
each flame a fresh prayer for her guru.
His mother laying down her needs
and melting into the vision of His holy feet.
Keerai Patti boiling greens with love
and tender care, refusing to taste a morsel
till she has fed her Master.
And o o o dear Lakshmi,
racing from the cowshed,
nudging English ladies aside
in her haste towards her darling
Ramana's ready lap, to feel His hand
patting her devoted, lowered head.

⤳ Plans ⤝

Ramana's tummy in trouble
so He decides to fast
and instead to do
Giripradakshina.
And as He walks,
He sees luminous lights
bobbing round Him
and then o god He hears
music of the Scriptures
and a half dozen women
looking for betel leaves,
who ask for directions.
As thanks, the first lady offers
some of her lunch, which
Ramana politely receives,
and then the second
raises a handful of rice.
Suddenly six women
offering Him food
He can't refuse.
And then, His devotee
Palanaswami comes round
the bend with special pepper juice
and mango - "nourishment
for the Master" - which He sups on.
And then o my! shuffling on,
He meets the ladies one more time.
They have no betel leaves
but it's supper now
and they want to feed Him.
Herbs and sweetmeats.

Despite his swelling belly,
He doesn't decline.
Six more meals he ingests,
helpless.
Filled to the crest,
He who had hoped
to empty
but in God's majesty,
He pats His stomach
and o so gently
smiles.

❧ Murugunar ❧

You may have been His shadow,
following His every move,
but the light He shed on you,
a thousand suns igniting
your o-so humble moon,
burned away all residue
of karma, and catapulted
you towards freedom,
to be the poetic scribe
of Truth, and surely lit
your path to the station
every time you couldn't
bear to leave Him
and had to be nudged
onto the train.
You, so devoted
to your mother too,
until she left her flesh
and you were free
to live in the stream
of His never ending
tenderness, and let
tears soak each page
you read to those
who chose to hear.
Hungry
to share all news
of Him, your own
Beloved, you served
Him well, and though
you talked to Him

ceaselessly even
when he left the room
and re-entered, your
sentences still flowing,
He heard the undeniable
Truth, your heart bursting
with devotion,
and He made pure
timeless, perfect
Poetry of you.

Arunachula Siva!

He first heard a line
in his head as he woke,
but kept going. Next
day, it still spoke
but now louder,
almost a song
swirling inside Him.
So He sat with His quill
and wove a garland,
sweet hymns of Heaven
for His Master,
the chorus of which
would ring through
Tiruvannamalai,
and years later,
that refrain He would hear
singing back to Him
through the door
as He lay on His death bed,
only hours left of His breath
enchanting the air,
and He wept
as He drank the tune He had given
now coming back for Him
on the wind
on the hill
on the lungs
of all who loved Him.

Poetry In Motion

The Garland of Arunachula,
Ramana's love poems to His guru,
kept Him and His devotees
in food for a long time.
Each day, the poems composed
in love for his Master's
delectation, would be taken
off the hill and into the
village, announced
by the blare
of the conch horn.
Arunachula Siva!
Arunachula Siva!
Arunachula Siva!
The people would hear
and come running with
offerings of sweet meats
and rice. The music
was magic gracing
the air and everyone
bowed to honor it.

IV.

THE SECOND DEATH AND RESURRECTION

Near Pachiamman Koil

After bathing in oils
with His attendants,
Ramana was overcome
by a curtain of white
sweeping across the horizon,
the world disappearing
and His body barely
breathing, skin cold,
blood blueing and
yet his I still thrived,
the Self still alive
and vibrant as He
heard Vasudeva crying:
a long lamentation
for his dead master,
until Master stood
back up, the curtain
parting and His beloved
mountain glowing gold
all around Him.

Full Moon

This is the day
that Ramana has His head
shaved as He sits on a stool
in the cowshed,
by his faithful barber,
scissors clipping
from behind
until
Ramana turns to the man,
commanding, *You sit!*
and folds into the floor,
making a perfect puddle
of His flesh
with the hay
and the animals.

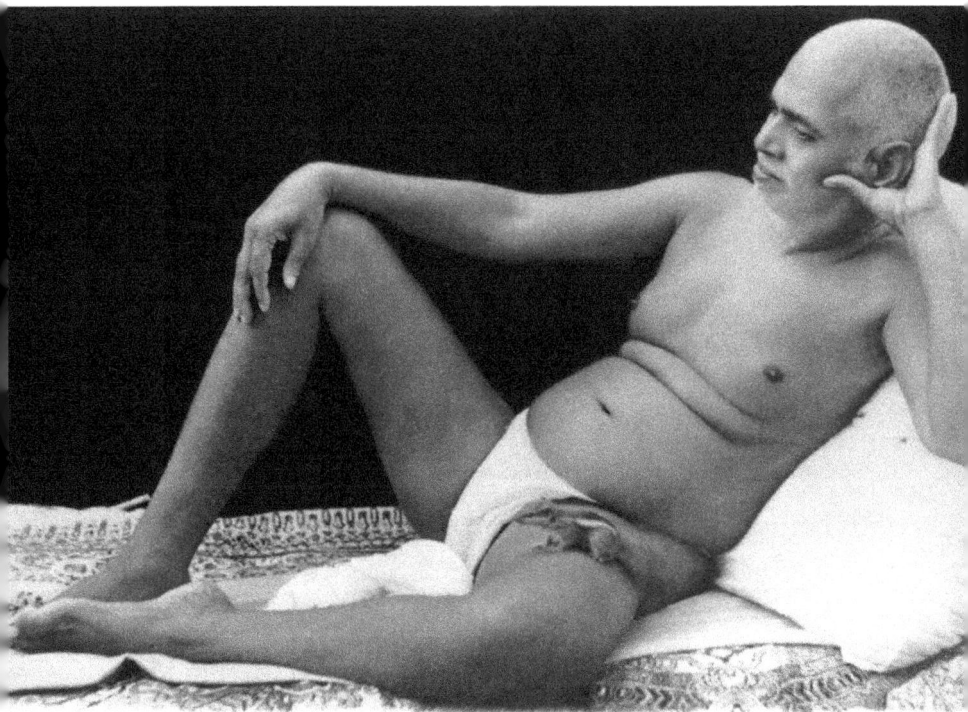

Singing

Ramana loved the birds
and squirrels, chipmunks
and dogs. He said
the monkeys could
do *tapas*, penance
to redeem themselves
in God's eyes, to draw
themselves closer
to His light. He stroked
and fed them
and felt concern
when He moved
down the mountain
to the ashram
in case His furry
feathered loved ones
would feel abandoned.
So He sent food up
the hill to them
with a firm invitation,
Come sit with me
whenever you need.
At my feet, all creatures
are always welcome.

What A Wonder!

Ramana reaching for His towel
knocked over the sparrow's nest
and o o o, one tiny egg split,
a long crack around the edge,
and Ramana fondled it and wept
and prayed for seven days
to the gods of healing.
"Let the crack be closed!
Oh, let the crack be closed!"
as He held the shattered shell
in His palms murmuring
soft words, as
He waited and prayed and
sang to the hidden bird.
And lo, one morning, He saw
the fissure sealed, made
new, born once more
in a glory of innocence
and He held it up
to the glad heavens
in delight, a joyous
schoolboy forgiven
for His sin of almost
taking life, *Look!*
What a wonder!
He proclaimed.

"She will hatch
after her fall,"
and sure enough,
a feather fluff appeared
at last, a sparrow
inching out from
under mother
and all rejoiced
as Ramana held her to
His lips and dropped
lover kisses, stroking
her warm fur
and showing everyone
who passed the miracle
of God's unending graces
in the most miniscule
of places.

"Their Gratitude, Only
They Could Know"

- Ramana

The ladies in their grass green saris
gather sheaves on the mountain
to feed their families, parched
in the dull heat of sun at high noon.
Backs bent in half to reach
each new stalk, their lips dry
and peeling, they move
in thin lines elegant
as a kingdom of ants,
yet they are not royalty.
Forbidden by caste
to drink of the one source
of water, they come to Ramana
almost in tears, crying,
Swami! Swami! Give us one sup.
And God, who knows no difference,
dips a pail into His well and pours it
over each stooped spine
in a fountain of love
so cool, so divine,
they all gasp in delight.

Some mornings, He conjures
an elixir of water, ginger
and light and raises the cup
to each woman's mouth
which they imbibe as if
it contained the one secret to life
- and it does:
a torrent of water dripping
down their delirious chins
and floating off each grateful finger.

❧ Porumda! ❧

That dog, all leaking sores,
all stinking fur, bone thin
and starving for
one taste of
his Master, one lick
of pure love,
was pushed and shoved
out of His orbit
time and again,
but ardor and passion
to touch the divine
is heard in the highest
reaches of heaven,
so that communion,
perfect, sublime
is granted to
the innocent,
regardless of looks
and so that wild animal's
lust was received
by the flesh of Ramana
one secret midnight,
when one tongue could
trawl the juicy map
of his God, from hair tip

to foot, and one dripping
sage could pick Himself
up, sparkling with dog love
and light, so one holy
wish now satisfied,
our dog could lie down
in great peace,
in gratitude, and die.

❧ Devotion ❧

Every day Ramana would sit out on a rock
to clean His teeth, even when the rains came
and the winds whipped at His *dhoti*,
still He sat, mountain and man fused
into The One, and when His devotees
tried to stop him, to lure Him towards
where it was warm, He refused.
It was years before they learned
the truth of His mission: an elderly
lady, He had heard, was no longer
able to walk to the ashram
and so she came within view
of His rock day after day.
Ramana, Lord of Lords,
how could He turn from
a true desire for *darshan*?

✿ Valli ✿

Mahdeva Swami promised
to take care of the deer
if Ramana would let her stay
so Valli moved into the ashram
and found her place at Master's feet.
She loved to nudge her head against His toes
while Ramana pushed back gently.
And when she rose on her hind legs,
Master followed, gleefully mirroring
her dance – the sage savoring animal antics.
And when her leg broke, He laid her next
to Him and rested one hand
on her head, the other on her heart.
Breathing softly, the twin forms melted
until she was ready to depart
her blood and skin and a shrine was built
to honor the life of the playful, blessed deer queen.

Annamalai Swami

Go to Palakottu,
Ramana told him,
and meditate alone.
Don't even think
of coming back.
Annamalai bowed his head
in reverence and in shock
and lugged his humble heart
to the western edge
of the ashram
and though he missed his Master
like an amputated arm,
though he longed to serve
his Beloved endlessly,
his surrender was so strong,
he turned his passion inward
to find the one source of Love.
Some days Ramana would kindly
come to visit so His boy
was not alone in his devotion
to the truth,
until he could look within
and find the Self revealed
to be not separate or apart
but Ramana in residence
as the radiance of his own
perfected heart.

Ramana In
Hollywood

Ramanatha Reddy with his cine camera
took 100 feet of film
of his beloved Master
and laid them out
on a white sheet
for all to view
but our dearest Ramana,
almost 70 years old then,
could not see
the images of His holy body
petting children,
His withered frame
shambling up the hill
and so they placed the sheet
against the window
by His sofa
and still He could not see
that mirage of form
moving round the ashram
pursued by a dozen devotees.
But did He care,
this beam of godlight,
when His heart all the while
gazed direct into infinity?

I Came For Your Sake

Collarbone broken as He tried
to save a squirrel from a dog,
body frail and waning as He
trailed uphill behind two men
to Skandashram. He came
to admire the stonemason's
quiet work, saying,
when He arrived,
"your prayers dragged
me here." And as I
read of such humble
tender love, the tears
could not be quenched
for He who was God
of Gods and o such
lover of men.

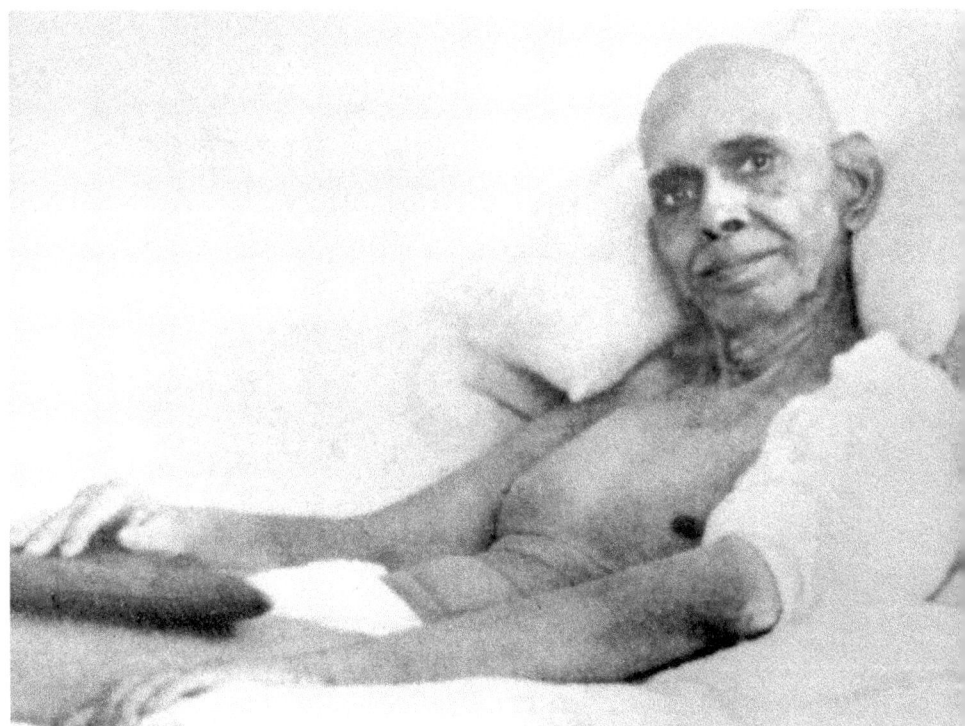

V.

FINAL DAYS

Reading

It all began last night,
tucking the story of Him
inside the pouch of my
chest, as I took with
me to sleep his left
arm dying, withered
with the weight of
pain sucked in,
His oozing arm
relieving endless
suffering with each
holy breath, His weeping
elbow freeing human grief
in a slow, timeless countdown,
o hollow bone, toward
April 14.

Ramana's Advice
On Jayanti

Why not mourn, He said,
a birthday? Why not grieve,
He suggested, your entry
into life, into this dream
of need and loss and strife?
Why not celebrate instead
the sweetness of your being
once the rusted, useless
machinery of mind has
lost its luster, has yielded
to being crushed into
oblivion, its absence
swinging wide the door
back into Heaven?

❧ Realization ❧

The wonder of this body!
You proclaimed towards
the end, sarcoma eating
up your bones. Half
laughing, You remarked
how a simple cough
was like lightning
ripping through
the sky. You,
whose body had
no horizons, one
flesh manifest
so man could
taste divine
in what it knew:
human skin
and blood.
You took on
our form
and let pain
overflood
to show us
the nature
of illusion,
how death
is not loss,
nor life, gain.

How we are
whole, entire,
regardless
of the frame.
How we need
to learn this
over and over
and yes, over
again.

Carry Me, He Said

Ramana in His final days,
shambling shuffling stuttering
towards me,
His feebling bones
blazing under cloth,
His walking stick
shaking under the limp
of His walk.
Carry Me, He said,
not on your shoulders,
not in your head.
Make a bower of your heart
so it may fill with the seeds
of my pleasure,
so all of my wounds
can flow through.
Let them breathe and release
so freedom may flower.
Carry Me, He said,
without need,
without measure.
And I will carry you.

The Holy Self

Pain doesn't touch Him
though He winces when
the doctor strains to remove
his tumor. The body has pain,
He says, but I am not that.
I am free of all suffering,
do what you like onto Me.
Soon I will be meeting
my father and bone-skin-
blood-history, leaving
only my True Essence.

Ramana's Last Supper

His final feast before He eased
out of the human garment,
before He slid across the sky
in a tapestry of light,
before He was consumed
into the True Beloved
was 3 teaspoons, delicately
placed on His sacred tongue
- o sweet communion! –
3 silver teaspoons of orange juice.

Ramana, Dying

The pain of nations tucked
under His arm, swelling
just below the elbow,
pus and blood and bone
could ruin anyone
but Him, who welcomes
all suffering inside His
perfect skin, which ripples
now in breathlike tides
over the rim of
separation, flooding
nothing but the dream
flesh, His holy heart wide
open to the predicament
of human wedded
to a form that does not
exist, as He will slowly,
quietly slip out of his
phantom robes, arms
luminous and limp,
the heavens trailing silver tears in the wake
of His ascension.

Ramana About ❧ To Die ❧

eyes staring into nowhere
the elbow, erupted flesh
feather in the wind
barely,
wings of His collarbones
long flown,
and only air
yielding
tetherless

Bedspread of
Death

Robed in a garment of air,
His eyes are pools that reflect
the cosmos. Grass in the wind
He is, mountain in pyramids
in the snow of His hair.
Who is it there in the picture,
billowing layer upon layer
of beauty so rare, it contains
multitudes in one form
about to melt
and spread across
galaxies like spilled
ink, spelling
Ramana Ramana
in a calligraphy of stars?

❧ Yes ❧

The peacocks,
my darling Ramana,
have all been fed,
by the grace of your love,
by your endless embrace,
fruit for all wounds,
so you can rest
as we can, too,
your hungry ones,
fed by the feast
of your tender,
unyielding gaze,
welcomed home
at last,
free of space,
into your exquisite
heart's nest.

Poem

Pradakshina With The King

Pradakshina With
The King

For a while Ramana let me be His walking stick
as He moved around His sacred hill,
o god, He could lean on me so beautifully
and He did, each step of His a miraculous
rhythm to which my being tuned and
when He sat, I tilted back and watched
the sky nourishing its clouds, His
palm all the while upon my head,
which in His care had become
a crown of jewels and lotuses,
rising up to Heaven's crest
above us and raining softly
down on man and wood
and mountain
all of it God's bounty
offered from His One Heart,
out of which all 'i' had
been carved, and hewn
now to bark and dust,
a bent branch hollowed
just enough to be allowed
to carry Him, gleaming
and hallowed by His handsome
and o unspeakably tender hand.

ACKNOWLEDGEMENTS

I bow to my beloved Ramana, whose exquisite grace gave birth to these poems. Line by line, He sang through my ear and my heart, a symphony floating onto the page. Gratitude is such a slight word to lay at the feet of The One who embodied silence.

And Holy Mountain, Arunachula, Ramana's guru, beacon of Light, destroyer of all that remains separate, needs no acknowledgment, though I am helpless but to offer it. As they say, God is the most humble of all.

My spiritual teacher and dear friend, David Waldman, deserves high praise. Without him, Ramana would never have flown into my life. He is the rarest of beings, devoting his days to luring us towards our divinity, while helping us embrace our humanness. I count my lucky stars for our meeting, and for learning, under his tender, unflinching tutelage, the gift of true love.

I am indebted to VS Ramanathan, President of Ramana Ashram, who kindly gave permission to use the archival photographs you see here, as well as encouragement with this book.

My heartiest thanks and awe go to Chris Quilkey, editor extraordinaire of the Mountain Path, the international publication devoted to Ramana. He has published many of the poems you have read here, as well as offering sage advice on the book. He went far beyond the call of duty in coordinating the photographs, and even provided several potential book covers, one of which graces this publication.

And dear Thayagu, deepest blessings on you, for your wonderful eye and sensibility in designing the book cover, as well as formatting the photographs. You made the job so easy. Thank you, thank you.

I offer profound gratitude to Prem Das Caulley, abiding, patient friend, who read the manuscript in its raw form and offered advice and warm support as often as it was needed.

Unspeakable appreciation goes to Marianne McGreevy, exceedingly generous spirit and utterly humble friend. After attending a poetry reading I gave on retreat, she slipped me a note, offering to completely fund the publication of The Boy Who Would Be Sage - a miracle beyond description. Her unparalleled kindness has led to this book you now hold in your hands. I will always be in her debt.

One last word of thanks goes to you, dear reader, for joining in this conversation of the Heart with Ramana. May His infinite love light your way too.

GLOSSARY

Alagammal, Venkataraman's birth mother, who eventually became his devotee and achieved samadhi upon her death

Annamalai Swami, Ramana's ardent devotee, who spent many years supervising building projects at Ramana Ashram

Arunachula, the holy mountain in southern India, to which Ramana was helplessly drawn after his awakening, and where he spent the rest of his life. He has said that his footsteps have covered every inch of that sacred hill

Asu Kavi, another name for Ganapati Muni

Brahman, the totality of God - The One into which all notions of God and Other are subsumed

Brahmana Swami, a name given to Venkataraman when He first arrived at Arunachula

Darshan, audience with a sage

Dhoti, Ramana's loincloth

Ganapati Muni, poet, sage, visionary. After years of intense penance and prayer, he approached Ramana for The Answer he had not yet found. Ramana ended years of silence in order to offer him what would become the revered technique of Self-Enquiry. It was he who gave Venkataraman the name Ramana, which translates, He Who Lives in The Heart of All Beings

Giripradakshina, circumambulation around Holy Mountain Arunachula, an act that is popular especially on the full moon, when one's sins can be expiated

Gurumurtum, a temple

Koundinya, a river in Tirichuzi

Murugunar, a supremely gifted poet who was profoundly devoted to Ramana

Nayana, can mean father or son, an affectionate term

Peacocks: Ramana's final words before he died were, "Have the peacocks been fed?"

Poppadum, Indian cracker or flatbread

Porumda! An exclamative that Ramana used, for which there is no literal translation

Prasad, offering of food to a guru

Sadhana, spiritual practice

Samadhi, the supreme state of Consciousness

Skandashram, Ramana's original ashram, uphill from Tiruvannamalai

Sundaram Iyer, Venkataraman's birth father

Tapas, penance

Tirichuzi, Venkataraman's boyhood town

Venkataraman, Ramana's boyhood name

Ana Ram Callan has been in love with Ramana since time immemorial.

www.ingramcontent.com/pod-product-compliance
Lightning Source LLC
LaVergne TN
LVHW091201080426
835509LV00006B/780